WORLD MYTHS
AND LEGENDS II

South America

Martha Schmitt

Fearon/Janus/Quercus
Belmont, CA
Simon & Schuster Education Group

World Myths and Legends
Greek and Roman
Ancient Middle Eastern
Norse
African
Far Eastern
Celtic
Native American
Regional American

World Myths and Legends II
India
Russia
Europe
South America
The Caribbean
Central America
Mexico
Southeast Asia

Series Editor: Joseph T. Curran
Cover Designer: Dianne Platner
Text Designer: Teresa A. Holden
Interior Illustrations: Mary Beth Gaitskill
Cover Photo: The Granger Collection, New York

Copyright © 1993 by Fearon/Janus/Quercus, a division of Simon & Schuster Education Group, 500 Harbor Boulevard, Belmont, CA 94002. All rights reserved. No part of this book may be reproduced by any means, transmitted, or translated into a machine language without written permission from the publisher.

Library of Congress Catalog Card Number: 92–72304
ISBN 0–8224–4645–6
Printed in the United States of America
2. 10 9 8 7 6 5 4
EB

CONTENTS

*An Introduction to the Myths
and Legends of South America*   v

1 In the Beginning

People from Stone
(Tiahuanacan of Peru)   1

Sun and Moon's Game
(Chamacoco of Paraguay)   7

How Night Began
(Bororo of Brazil)   11

People from the Sky
(Warao of Venezuela)   14

The Great Flood
(Ayoreo of Bolivia)   18

2 How Things Came to Be

Children of the Sun
(Inca of Peru)   25

The Tree of Food
(Yaruro of Venezuela)   31

The Twins *(Carib of Guyana)*	37
The Fisherman and the Fish *(Trio of Brazil)*	42
The Boy and the Jaguar *(Cayapo of Brazil)*	48
The Man Who Made the Plains *(Cuiva of Colombia)*	58

3 Animals and People

The Bird Woman *(Inca of Peru)*	63
The Man Who Caught Too Many Fish *(Kariña of Venezuela)*	68
The Otter Woman *(Cuiva of Colombia)*	72
The Condor's Wife *(Inca of Peru)*	76
The Jaguar's Wife *(Chamacoco of Paraguay)*	83
The Rabbit's Trick *(Warao of Guyana)*	93
The Red Birds *(Mataco of Argentina)*	97

Pronunciation Guide — 101

An Introduction to the Myths and Legends of South America

South America is a large continent. It has a great variety of plants and animals. The continent has been home to many groups of people, in fact, hundreds of groups. From their varied environments have come a rich store of myths and legends.

The powerful Incas made up one group who have lived in South America. In the 1400s, the Incas ruled a large empire. It included some of present-day Colombia, Ecuador, Peru, Bolivia, Chile, and Argentina. In the highlands of Peru, there are still groups of people whose language and ceremonies are similar to those of the old Inca culture.

Some groups were wiped out after the Europeans arrived on the continent. In other cases, native cultures became mixed with elements from European cultures. In South America today, there are some groups of people who still follow very old traditional ways of life.

In many places in South America, stories have been passed on through the years by storytellers. In villages of the past, people would gather around a storyteller in the evening. The storyteller would talk in a lively way, sometimes even acting out parts of a story. The stories were told to entertain, as well as to pass on beliefs and customs. Today, in some South American villages, storytellers continue to entertain audiences with amazing tales.

The myths and legends of South America are full of unusual events. In one story, for example, gods arise from a lake and travel on the earth. In some stories, the sun and the moon are people and have adventures on the earth. In others, people turn into animals, and animals turn into people. In these stories, animals and people mix freely, talking and living with one another.

Many of the stories in this book are told in several South American countries. Some stories have a lot of versions, with different events and often different endings.

This book presents a sampling of the many thousands of South American myths and legends. As you read the myths, imagine yourself listening to a storyteller in a South American village.

People from Stone

Long ago the people of ancient Peru believed that the god Viracocha created the world and its people. This is a story told by the Tiahuanacan. It tells about the beginning of the world. In the story, Viracocha creates people from stone, a common material in the mountainous country of Peru.

The First People

In the beginning, there was only the darkness. Then Viracocha came forth from Lake Titicaca and formed the earth and the skies. He then made animals and a group of giant people.

These giant people did not please Viracocha. They were thoughtless and unkind. The ways of the giant people angered the god so much that he destroyed them all. He also destroyed all the animals and every other living thing.

Viracocha continued to create parts of the world, though. His power was great. Viracocha created everything with just a wave of his hand and a word. He created day by making the sun rise up from an island in Lake Titicaca. He created the moon and stars. He set each form of light on its own path. He created streams and rivers. He made and moved mountains and valleys.

Viracocha decided to make animals to replace the ones he had destroyed. He first made birds to fly in the sky and fill the air with song. He gave a different song to each type of bird. He sent some birds to live in the mountains and some to live in the valleys. Then Viracocha created the animals that walked on four legs and those that crawled on their bellies. As he had with the birds, he sent the animals to live in the mountains and in the valleys.

Viracocha Makes People Once More

After creating the animals, Viracocha began once more to make people. He used stone to form men, women, and children. Then he painted them as he wanted them to look.

Some of the stone women were pregnant. Other stone women were already caring for young children in cradles. He painted on the clothing that each person would wear. Viracocha fashioned the people as they would

Stone people

be in life. Then he created a stone village in Tiahuanaco for some of the stone people to live in.

Viracocha divided the stone people into groups. He gave each group its own foods, its own language, and its own songs. Then he directed all the stone people to sink underground. He ordered them to stay underground until he or one of his helpers called them.

Then Viracocha gathered his helpers who had risen with him from Lake Titicaca. He said to them, "Some of you walk south, some walk west, and the others walk toward the morning sun. Divide the lands among yourselves. After you arrive in your own land, call forth the stone people from under the ground."

The helpers did as Viracocha directed. One by one, the groups of stone figures came up from the ground.

Viracocha walked north toward the future city of Cuzco. As he walked, he gave life to each group of people, as did his helpers. Viracocha said to them, "I command human beings to come out from these stone figures. Live on this land! Live here, and have your children."

Viracocha and his helpers showed the people how to live on earth. They told these new people the names of trees and other plants. They taught the people which plants were good for eating. They taught them which plants were good for healing and which plants would cause sickness and death. Viracocha gave instructions for the people to be kind, to respect one another, and to live in peace.

The End of the Journey

After he had made the stone people come to life, Viracocha continued walking and teaching. Once he came to a group of people who carried rocks. They did not recognize Viracocha, and they threw the rocks at him. This made Viracocha angry, but he did not destroy them. He made fire fall from the sky onto the people. At once, the people put down their rocks and dropped to the ground at Viracocha's feet. Viracocha then put out the fire and explained to the people that he was their creator.

When they heard this, the people built a large stone statue of Viracocha. With this statue, the people thanked the god who had made them. They set the statue at the spot where Viracocha had caused the fire to fall. They offered gold and silver to honor the god. Ever since that time, people have continued to place gold and silver at that sacred place in honor of Viracocha.

At last, Viracocha was at the end of his journey in the world. Since his work on earth was completed, he went back to the water. His helpers joined him, and they walked out into the ocean.

The people watched in wonder. Viracocha and his helpers walked upon the sea as though it were land!

Viracocha and his helpers kept walking on the sea toward the setting sun. It was the last time the people ever saw Viracocha.

The people said the creator was named Viracocha because *Viracocha* meant "foam of the sea."

1. *What did Viracocha make people from?*
2. *How did the people find out which plants they could eat?*
3. *Why is the creator named Viracocha?*

Sun and Moon's Game

> *This myth is from the Chamacoco of Paraguay. In this myth and many other South American stories, Sun and Moon roamed the earth as people. The story explains why the sun shines during the day and the moon shines at night. Unlike many stories, it presents the moon as more important than the sun.*

One morning, Sun said to Moon, "Today let's have some fun. Let's go to the water and change into fish. We will see which of us is stronger."

When they got to the water, Sun told Moon that he was going to become an eel.

"I'm going to be the thinnest type of eel," said Sun. "I'll stay under the water as long as I can. Then you can change into an eel, and we'll see who can stay under longer. Whoever can make the most air bubbles will win. That one will be the stronger."

Sun jumped into the water, while Moon waited on the bank. Sun changed into an eel, and his breathing made an air bubble. Moon tried to stop Sun's air bubble by pressing down on it with his hand and foot. Even so,

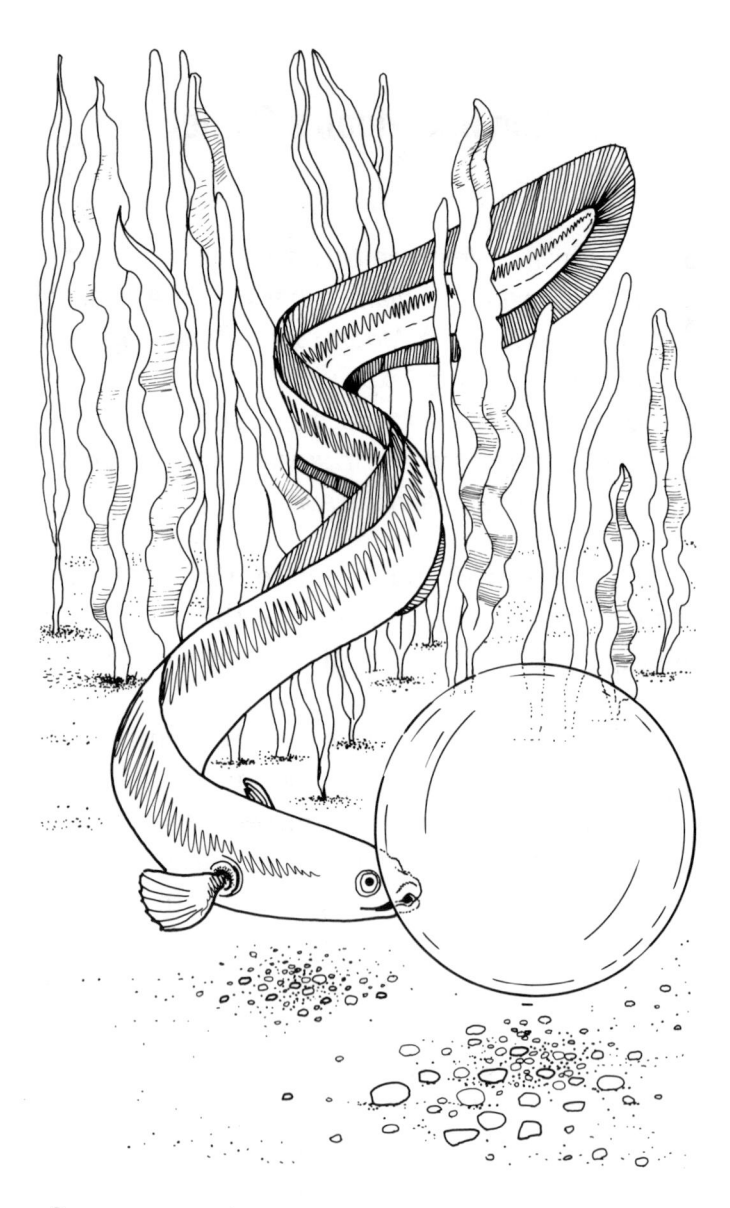

Sun as an eel

Sun was able to keep breathing, and he made four air bubbles.

Then Moon grabbed the eel's head and pulled him up. Sun's turn was over. Moon threw the eel on the land, and Sun changed into a person again.

"Now it's your turn to become an eel," Sun said.

Moon made himself become the biggest type of eel and disappeared. When Sun saw the air bubbles, he covered them, trying to stop Moon's breathing. Moon was still able to make six air bubbles.

Then Moon jumped out of the water while Sun was still pressing down. Moon became a person again and stood behind Sun, where Sun couldn't see him.

Finally, Moon laughed and spoke. He said, "Look around, Sun. I'm already out of the water. I won! I made more air bubbles than you did."

Sun said, "Yes, you won. You are stronger. So you will take the harder job of lighting the sky at night. I'll light up the sky during the day, and you'll do it at night. When there are clouds at night, people will still be able to see because of your strong light."

Moon said, "All right, we'll have one kind

of light for night and another kind for day. The moon will shine at night, and the sun will shine in the day. Those are the jobs we will have."

Then Moon went on. "When it rains, no one will be able to see you, even in all your brightness. My light will be stronger. At night, people will be able to see, even when there are clouds. The clouds won't hide my light as they do yours."

Then Sun and Moon rose to the sky.

There is no sunshine when it rains because Moon decided it should be so. At night there is always some light, even when it rains, because Moon was stronger.

1. *What kind of animal did Sun and Moon change into?*
2. *How did Moon prove he was stronger than Sun?*
3. *Why did the winner get to light up the sky at night?*

How Night Began

In this myth from the Bororo of Brazil, Sun is once again a person. The myth tells how Sun came to have power over the night.

Sun was owner of the light. He wanted it to be day all the time. Heron, a large bird, was owner of the darkness.

One day, Sun visited Heron's nest. It had two baby birds in it.

"Where is Heron?" Sun thought. "Heron should be home when I visit. I will punish Heron by killing his children." Then Sun grabbed the mouths of the young birds and ripped them apart. The birds died.

Soon after Sun had left, Heron returned from fishing. Heron saw his dead children and was sad and angry. In his grief, he brought out the darkness and made night fall.

Sun was afraid of the darkness, and he began to cry. Heron heard Sun's cries and felt sorry for him. He took back the darkness and flew toward the sound of Sun's crying.

When Heron found Sun, he said, "The darkness was for my sorrow. What happened to my children? Sun, did you kill my precious children?"

"No," said Sun, "I did not."

Heron did not believe Sun. Once more Heron made the earth dark, and again Sun cried out.

Again Heron asked, "Did you kill my little ones, Sun?"

Once again, Sun answered with a lie. "No, I did not," he said.

Sun did not tell the truth because he thought he could make a deal with Heron. Sun hoped that Heron would ask for help. Then Sun could ask Heron for a favor in return. He wanted to ask Heron to give him power over the night.

Heron seemed to read Sun's mind.

"Oh, Sun," said Heron, "please bring my children back to life. If you do this for me, I'll make you the ruler of the night."

"Yes, I will gladly help you," Sun said.

So Sun took some sap from a tree. He used the sap to glue white feathers on the wounded mouths of the young birds. These white feathers patched the mouths. Then he blew on the baby birds. Sun's breath brought the dead birds back to life.

Heron hugged his children with joy.

"Thank you, Sun," he said. "Now I will give you the night. Now you shall have power over darkness! I must ask you one thing, however. When I feel sad and call out, help me by taking away the darkness. Will you do this favor for me?"

"Yes, I will," Sun promised.

Ever since that time, white feathers have grown at the corners of the heron's beak. Ever since then, the Sun rules the night. Sun decides when darkness will come. Also, ever since then, the heron sings at sunrise to thank the sun.

1. *What did Heron do when he saw his dead children?*
2. *What was the last thing Sun did to bring the dead birds back to life?*
3. *Why does the heron sing at sunrise?*

People from the Sky

The Warao of Venezuela tell this story about the first people on the earth. In it, the first people come to the earth from the sky. They climb down through a hole created by a shaman, a kind of religious or spiritual leader.

In the beginning, people did not live on the earth. They lived in the sky.

One day, one of the people, a shaman, shot an arrow into the air. The arrow rose in the air and then fell down onto the floor of the sky. There the arrow made a hole in the floor of the sky.

The shaman pulled out the arrow, but then sand began to pour through the hole. The sand swirled through the hole, making the hole larger.

The hole in the sky became so large that people could look through it to the earth below. When the people saw the mountains, oceans, and rivers, they became excited. They sent a small group of people down to the earth to explore.

One man climbed down to the earth on a

The hole in the sky

rope made from palm-tree fibers. He landed on an island of the Orinoco Delta. He explored the whole island and then returned to his people in the sky.

The man told his people, "The earth is wonderful. Water surrounds it. There are many fish, animals, and palm trees."

"Then we should go down to the earth and live there," the people said.

They decided on a day to make the journey to the earth. Then they made a special rope just for this purpose. When the day came, the people began to climb down the rope, one by one.

The last two people to go were the shaman and his wife. Just as the shaman was about to climb down, his wife asked to go first. His wife was very large because she was in the last month of her pregnancy. She tried and tried to get through the hole, but it was too narrow for her.

The shaman pushed and pushed his wife. He even jumped on top of her trying to get her through. The pushing and jumping did not help, though. The woman could only get one of her legs through the hole.

The leg of the shaman's wife stayed in the hole, closing the opening to the sky forever.

The woman's leg is still there, but it was changed into seven stars. This group of stars forms the constellation of the Great Bear, also known as the Big Dipper. The Warao call this group of stars No-hi-ha-basi.

The people from the sky always remembered the woman whose leg was stuck in the hole in the sky. They remembered her whenever they looked up and saw the stars of the Great Bear.

1. *Where did people live in the beginning?*
2. *Why did the people want to come to the earth?*
3. *How was the opening in the sky closed?*

The Great Flood

Many tribes in South America tell stories about a great flood that occurred long ago. In most of these myths, only a few people live through the flood. After the flood, life starts over again on the earth. In this myth from the Ayoreo of Bolivia, lightning becomes a boy who brings the great flood.

One morning a man went into the forest to look for honey. As he was walking, he suddenly heard a loud crashing noise. He ran toward the sound and came across a young boy with long hair. The boy was lying on the ground. He was trying to get up, but he couldn't. His legs were stuck in the ground, and he was weak and sick.

Although the man was afraid, he went up to the boy. He thought of the loud sound as he looked into the boy's face. Then the man realized that the boy was Lightning.

"What's wrong?" asked the man.

"I hit a tree and fell," said Lightning. "I hurt myself. Please help me! If you take care of me, I will go home with you and become your son. You can be my father."

Lightning stuck in the ground

"All right," the man said, "I will help you."

So the man dug the boy out of the ground. He lifted Lightning up and carried the boy to his camp where his wife was. He told his wife what had happened, and she agreed that they would take care of Lightning.

The man and woman treated the boy like a son. They knew that Lightning was different from other boys, however. For that reason, they kept the boy with them all the time. They did not let him play with the other boys. They were afraid the other boys would hurt him because he would seem strange to them.

The man often took the boy along to hunt for food in the forest. One day, they were out looking for honey. By the time they found a tree with honey, the man was thirsty. He told the boy to go find a *cipoi,* a plant that had water inside it. The boy did as he was told and returned with a small cipoi.

The man squeezed the cipoi and collected the water from it in a jar. He got only a small amount of water, which he drank.

Then the man said, "I am still thirsty. Where can we get some more water?"

While the man was looking away, Lightning quickly squeezed his long hair and water came out. The water from his hair filled the jar.

"Here is some water, Father," said Lightning. Then he handed the jar to his father.

The man took the water and drank it. He thought to himself, "This is strange. Where did my son get this water?" The man did not ask the boy, though, because he had decided to find out another way.

The next day the man took Lightning into the forest again to hunt for honey. After a short time, they came to a tree with honey. Again, the man said he was thirsty and sent Lightning to find a cipoi.

While Lightning was gone, the man climbed up the tree, using a rope. When the boy returned with a cipoi, the man was sitting near the top of the tree. "From up here, I will watch to see what the boy does," thought the man.

The man said to the boy, "Fill the jar with water, and then I will come down."

The man watched as the boy squeezed the cipoi. The plant did not have enough water to fill the jar, though. The boy looked up to make sure his father was not looking. The man pretended to be collecting honey.

However, as the boy squeezed water out of his hair, the man sneaked a glance.

"This is very strange," thought the father. "This boy can make water!"

A few days passed before the man went back to gather honey. This time he did not bring the boy along.

The other boys in the camp asked Lightning to play with them. The boys were playing a game they often played. As part of this game, they kicked one another.

"I will play with you in a little while," Lightning told the boys. Then he started to build a hut.

After the hut was finished, Lightning began to play with the boys. They played their game of kicking. Lightning did not enjoy the game at all.

"Don't kick me," he said. The boys did not listen. One of the boys kicked Lightning again.

Some strange things began to happen. Lightning raised his arms. Flashes of lightning shot out from his armpits. Suddenly thunder sounded and rain began to fall. The rain got heavier and heavier.

Lightning ran into the hut he had built. As the water rose all around, the hut floated on the water. Lightning would not let the other boys come into the hut.

"You were not nice to me. I will not let you in my house," Lightning said.

Then more strange things happened. Lightning changed the boys and the other people in the camp into toads and frogs. They were not able to get into the hut where it was dry. Lightning wanted to save his earthly mother and father, however. So he gave them the power to walk on water. By walking on the water, they would be able to get to the hut and escape the flood.

"Come into my house," Lightning called to his earthly parents. "You will be safe here."

The man and woman reached the hut safely. As the flood waters rose, Lightning's real father and mother took him back up to the sky. In time, Lightning made the rain on earth stop.

The husband and wife were the only ones on earth to live through the flood. They were saved because they had been kind to Lightning.

From these two people have come all those who now live on earth.

1. Why couldn't Lightening get up from the ground at first?
2. How did Lightning produce water for his earthly father to drink?
3. What kind of game were the boys playing?

Children of the Sun

The Incas lived in the Andes Mountains of Peru and built a great empire during the 1400s. Their tribal god was the sun. This myth tells about their first rulers and the beginning of the Inca Empire. The Incas called their king the Inca and their queen the Coya.

Long ago the earth was wilderness, and the people on it lived like wild animals. The people did not have houses or farms or villages. They lived in caves or under whatever shelter they could find. They ate wild fruits, roots, and other plants. Sometimes they ate the flesh of other people. They used leaves, bark, and animal furs to cover their bodies. Some people went without clothes.

Father Sun felt that the people should not live like animals. He decided to send his son the Inca and daughter the Coya to teach the people how to live better. Father Sun wanted his children to show people how to grow crops and build houses. He also wanted them to give the people laws for living and to teach them to worship the sun.

Father Sun sent his children to Lake Titicaca and told them to go from there in any direction. He gave them a golden rod. The rod was two fingers thick and shorter than a person's arm. Father Sun told his children to push the rod into the ground wherever they stopped to eat or sleep. If the rod went into the ground with one push, they should establish a city in that spot. They would become rulers of that city.

Father Sun said to his children, "You will be rulers of all the people. Rule wisely and fairly and with kindness. Treat the people the way loving parents would treat their children."

Father Sun told the Inca and the Coya that they must be like him. He said, "I take care of the earth, giving it light and warmth. I make rain. I make the pastures green, I make the trees grow fruit, and I make the livestock bear young. I cross the sky each day to see what the people need and to help and comfort them."

The children listened as their father continued to explain. He said, "You must help these people who now live like animals. I will make you rulers over all the people. Lift them up with your good teaching."

Then Father Sun's children walked north from Lake Titicaca. Wherever they stopped, they tried to push the golden rod into the ground. Everywhere, however, the soil was rocky, and the rod would not go down.

At last they came to the Valley of Cuzco, which was then still a wilderness. They stopped at the hill that is now called Rainbow. There they pushed the rod into the earth. With one thrust it disappeared, for the soil was not rocky.

The Inca said to his sister the Coya: "Father Sun has ordered us to build a city here. We must do as he commands. You go in one direction, and I will go in another. We will gather all the people and tell them what to do. We will begin our father's work."

Then the Inca went north, and the Coya went south. As they traveled, they talked to the people they found.

This is what they said: "Father Sun has sent us from the sky to be rulers over you. We will lead you out of the wilderness. We will show you how to raise crops. We will teach you how to live in towns." The people were amazed at the fine clothes Father Sun's children wore. The Inca and the Coya also had pierced ears, which the people had never

The Inca and the Coya with the golden rod

seen before. The people believed that these were indeed Sun's children. The people wanted the things that their rulers, the Inca and the Coya, promised.

So the people formed a large group and followed the children of Sun to Cuzco. The rulers ordered some people to grow crops in the fields. They told others to make houses. This is how Cuzco was built and came to be filled with people.

After the city was built, the Inca showed people how to work. He taught them how to plant crops. He showed them how to make plows and other farming tools. He taught them how to make canals to water their fields. The Inca even showed them the way to make shoes.

At the same time, the Coya taught people. She showed them how to spin cotton and wool, how to weave cloth, and how to sew clothes.

The people saw how much their lives had improved. They went joyfully to tell others the good news. They wore their new clothes and brought along their new foods. They told the other people about their new houses.

Many more people came out of the wilderness to find out if the stories were true. They saw for themselves that all they had heard was true. Then they joined the others in obeying and serving the Inca and the Coya. In a few years, many people had been joined together under the rule of the Inca and the Coya.

This was how Cuzco and the great Inca Empire began. The children of Sun were the first rulers, and the later rulers came from them.

1. Why did Father Sun feel the people on the earth needed his son and daughter?
2. Whom did Father Sun send to teach the people?
3. What was the first city to be built?

The Tree of Food

This story comes from the Yaruro of Venezuela. It tells about a magic tree that grows all types of food. The myth explains how people first came to grow crops.

The people in the story are criollos, *a name for Spanish Americans. The main character in the story is Tapir. A tapir is a South American animal that looks somewhat like a pig. The story also mentions some special foods. Mangos and plantains are tropical fruits. Manioc is a root that can be eaten. Manioc is a basic food in South America. It is used to make a type of flat bread or cake.*

A long time ago, the people called criollos lived on the plains. Because they did not have all the foods they have today, they ate mostly wild roots and birds. The criollos were often hungry because food was sometimes hard to find.

In the forest was a huge food tree named Tohurato. All kinds of foods grew on the tree. The people did not know about Tohurato, however.

Tohurato, the tree of food

The Tree of Food

Tapir, who was then a man, was the only person who knew about Tohurato. Every day Tapir visited Tohurato and ate some of the fruit from the tree.

One day Tapir walked back into his village after eating some fruit from Tohurato. One of the villagers asked Tapir, "What were you eating? You smell sweet."

Tapir had eaten bananas and mangos and plantains and sugarcane, but he did not tell the villager. He would not tell the other people anything about the tree.

After a time, the people in the village began to wonder where Tapir got his food. While they were hungry, Tapir was always well fed. Whenever anyone asked him about food, Tapir would say that he had not been eating.

The people were not fooled, however. They talked among themselves, and one day they decided to follow Tapir. When Tapir left the village, the people sneaked after him, staying far behind.

After a while, Tapir spotted the people following him. He ran into the forest and went straight to Tohurato. The people rushed after him. They found Tapir at the food tree.

The people were amazed. The huge tree

had all types of fruits and vegetables on it.

The people said to Tapir, "So this is where you get your food. You were keeping this tree a secret."

Tapir answered, "I cannot deny it. You have caught me."

Then the people started to taste all the different fruits. They decided to cut the tree down so that they could take the manioc, plantain, corn, and other foods with them.

The people told Tapir, "Cut down the tree so that we can bring all this food back to the village."

Tapir started to chop down the tree with an axe. He kept chopping and chopping, but the tree was so big he couldn't cut it down. He knew that he needed help.

Tapir turned to Woodpecker who was nearby. "Woodpecker, will you help me?" asked Tapir. "I will give you some food if you help me cut down the tree." So Woodpecker starting pecking at the tree with his beak. Tapir and Woodpecker worked at the tree for a long time. Finally they felled the tree.

Then the people said to Tapir, "Get a big basket to put all this food in. We need something to carry the bananas, corn, watermelons, squash, pineapples, manioc, and plantains. Go straight to the village and get a huge basket."

While Tapir headed toward the village, the people sorted the food. They made a pile of each type.

Although Tapir tried to go straight to the village, he got lost. He was gone for two days before he found his way to the village.

When Tapir did get there, he picked out the biggest basket he could find. Then he returned to the food tree where the people were waiting.

"Fill the basket with all the food, Tapir. We'll take it home," they said. "We have a lot of food because we have picked all the while you were gone."

Tapir did as he was told. Then the people took the basket back to their village.

The people were able to grow new crops by planting some of the food they had brought home. From then on they had many kinds of food. They did not have to eat just wild roots and birds.

Tapir and the Tohurato tree had provided a new way of life.

1. Where did Tapir go to eat?
2. Why did the criollos tell Tapir to cut down the tree?
3. Who helped Tapir cut down the tree?

The Twins

Many South American tribes tell stories about twin heroes. In this myth from the Carib of Guyana, the twin heroes give people a way to make fire.

One day Sun started out on a journey. His wife, who was pregnant with twins, tried to follow him. However, she could not keep up with him.

At first one of the twins helped guide his mother. The baby spoke to his mother from inside her body, telling her which way to go.

As Sun's wife was walking, a wasp landed on her belly. The woman hit the wasp, shaking the children inside her. The twin who had been guiding her became angry. He would not speak to his mother anymore, and so she did not know which way to go.

In a short time, the woman started to go the wrong way. She took a path that led to Frog's house. Now Frog was a big, old woman.

When the woman came to the house, Frog said, "Hello there! What are you doing here?"

The woman answered, "I was following

my husband, but I couldn't keep up with him. I am lost now, and I am very tired. Can you help me?"

"Come in then," said Frog. "You can rest here. I will give you something to eat and drink."

"Oh, thank you," said the woman, as she entered Frog's house.

Frog gave the woman some food and drink and then sat down next to her. Frog asked, "Will you please pick the lice from my head?"

"Oh, yes," the woman answered. "I would be happy to return your kindness."

The woman started to remove the lice from Frog's head. It was the custom to bite lice to kill them. However, Frog told the woman, "Do not bite the lice. The lice can poison you if you put them in your mouth."

After a while, the tired woman forgot what Frog had said. She put one of the lice in her mouth to bite it. As soon as she bit it, she died.

Quickly Frog cut open the woman's belly. She took out the twins, two beautiful boys.

The Boys Live with Frog

Frog took care of the babies and raised

them with love. In time, the boys grew bigger. Soon they were big enough to hunt birds. They also started to catch fish to eat.

However, a strange thing would happen each time they brought some fish to Frog.

"Go get some wood for the fire. Then I can cook the fish," Frog would say.

Following Frog's orders, the boys would go into the forest to hunt for wood. When they returned, they'd find the fish already cooked.

"I wonder how this happens," said one of the twins to the other. "Each time we come back, the fish are already cooked. We never see any fire. How does Frog do this?"

"I will find out how she does it," said the other twin. The next time the twins brought home fish, the one boy changed himself into a lizard. He crawled up under the roof of the house to watch the old woman.

As he watched, Frog spit some fire out of her mouth. She cooked the fish over the fire. After the fish was cooked, she swallowed the fire again. As the boy watched in wonder, Frog also drained a milklike liquid from her neck. Then she used the liquid to make manioc flour.

Later the boy told his brother all that he

had seen. They both thought these things were very strange. The boys were suddenly afraid of Frog.

"I do not trust the old woman," said one of the twins to the other. "She might be planning to cook us as she cooks the fish. I think we should kill her."

The brothers agreed to kill the woman. They took Frog to the middle of a large field. They took some wood called *hima-heru* and placed it all around her. Finally, they rubbed the sticks of wood and started a fire. The old woman began to burn.

Soon, Frog was completely burned up. After that the threat of the old woman was gone. The twins felt they were safe.

The twins also had found a way to make fire by using the hima-heru wood.

Because of this fire, people found that they could all make fire easily. They could use the hima-heru wood because it would burn easily.

Since that time, people rub two pieces of hima-heru wood together to make fire.

1. *How did the woman shake the twins inside her?*
2. *What did Frog do when the woman died?*
3. *Why did the twins kill Frog?*

The Fisherman and the Fish

This myth comes from the Trio of Brazil. It tells how the Trio first learned to plant crops, to make cooking tools, and to bake bread.

Paraparawa Meets Waraku

Paraparawa was a fisherman. One day, while fishing in a river, he caught a waraku, a small fish. The fish jumped out of Paraparawa's hands and disappeared.

All of a sudden, Paraparawa heard a woman's voice calling to him. It said, "Hello, Paraparawa." It was the fish, Waraku, who had become a woman so she could talk to the man.

Paraparawa was surprised. He spoke timidly to the woman standing there. "What do you want?"

"I do not want to be eaten," said the woman. "I want to go to your village and see where you live."

Paraparawa explained that his village was just a simple place. Waraku still wanted to go there. So the two of them walked to Paraparawa's village.

When they reached the village, Paraparawa explained, "I do not have a house. I sleep under the stars, out in the reeds. The reeds also serve as my food. I eat their soft center, which is juicy. You see, my needs are simple."

"Fine," said Waraku. "You have told me what I wanted to know."

Then the two of them went back to the river. At the riverbank, Waraku said, "Do not go away yet. My father is bringing some food that I want you to see."

Standing on the riverbank, Paraparawa saw the head of a giant alligator in the water. Its mouth was full of plants. The alligator swam toward Paraparawa and Waraku. As the animal got closer, Paraparawa was filled with fear and fled.

When he was far enough away to feel safe, Paraparawa stopped and looked back. He saw the alligator come up on the shore. The animal dropped some green plants by Waraku and went back into the river.

Waraku called, "Come back, Paraparawa. The alligator is my father, and he has brought food for you. He will not hurt you."

Paraparawa went back to the riverbank. Then Waraku said to him, "I give these

The alligator bringing food

plants to you. From this day on, you will have this good food. This food tastes much better than the reed. Here are yams and sweet potatoes and bananas. This is the yucca, which has a thick root you can eat. You can also drink from the yucca."

"I thank you. I don't know how to eat these plants, though. Besides, after they are gone, what do I do?"

Waraku told him, "You don't eat these plants as they are now. You put them in the soil and let them grow. Then you eat them. Never eat a whole plant, though. Always save a part of each plant to put in the soil. Then let that part grow. In this way, you will always have more plants. I will show you how to get a field ready and how to plant fruits and vegetables."

Waraku showed the fisherman how to clear land and how to plant each type of crop. Paraparawa planted each type of food in its own row.

After they had finished planting, Waraku said, "Now just keep the weeds out of this field. These plants need only sunlight and rain, and they will grow quickly. After the fruits and vegetables ripen, I will come back and show you what to do. For now, just work here every morning, and soon I will return."

Paraparawa went back with Waraku to the river. As he watched, she jumped into the water and became a fish again. Then Paraparawa went back to his field and sat down to think about everything that had happened.

The Plants Are Successful

Each morning Paraparawa went to his field. He could see that the plants from Waraku were growing bigger. With a happy heart, the fisherman worked to pull out the weeds that grew up in the field. After a number of weeks, the leaves on his plants grew very big.

For many mornings, Paraparawa worked in his field alone. Finally, one morning, Waraku was there when Paraparawa arrived. She was a woman again and had come to help the fisherman.

Waraku stayed for a while. She showed the fisherman how to make cooking tools and how to cook all the new foods.

These new foods were very different to Paraparawa. He had to get used to eating them and had to learn to like them. At first, he even had a hard time swallowing the foods. Waraku told him to keep trying.

"In time you will like these foods better than the reed," Waraku said.

What Waraku said was true. Paraparawa soon grew to like the new foods, and the reed no longer tasted good to him.

After a while, Paraparawa did not eat the reed at all. There was plenty of new food. Each food had a special taste, and each food was good.

1. *How did Paraparawa first meet Waraku?*
2. *What new plants did the alligator bring?*
3. *Who taught Paraparawa how to grow the plants and how to cook the food from them?*

The Boy and the Jaguar

> The Cayapo of Brazil tell a different story about how people got fire and food crops. The jaguar, a large, wild cat of South America, plays an important part in this story.

The Boy Meets the Jaguar

Long ago, people did not have fire. They did not have roasted meat or baked manioc cakes. They had no bananas or sweet potatoes. They baked meat on stones in the sun. They ate only the fruit they found in the forest. The people did not have thread for sewing either.

One morning, a man took his brother-in-law, who was very young, into the forest. They came upon a large rock. On top of the rock, some birds were nesting. The man found a big log and propped it against the rock. Then the boy climbed up to get the young birds from the nest.

As the boy reached into the nest, a rock fell and hit his brother-in-law below. The rock broke one of the man's fingers. Angry, the man pushed the big log away from the rock and went home. The young boy was left on top of the rock and could not get down.

About noon, a big jaguar came by the rock. He was returning home from hunting. On his back he carried game he had killed. The load of game was so heavy that the jaguar was panting. The young boy heard the jaguar. He leaned over to see who was going by. The boy's shadow fell in front of the jaguar and surprised the animal.

The jaguar raised his head and saw the boy on the rock above.

"Why are you up there?" the jaguar asked the boy.

"My brother-in-law left me here. I have no way to get down," the boy answered.

The jaguar saw the big log. He picked it up and placed it against the rock again.

"Here's a log," he told the boy. "Now you can climb down."

The boy started to climb down the trunk. As he came down, he looked at the jaguar. He saw the animal's big head and sharp teeth. The boy was frightened and hurried back up to the top of the rock.

"I'm afraid you'll eat me," said the boy.

"No. I promise I won't hurt you. Come on down," the jaguar answered.

The jaguar finding the boy

Twice more the boy started down the trunk but climbed back up in fear.

Then the jaguar said, "Look, I'll take you to my home. There, I will take good care of you. I'll give you all the meat you can eat. I have game and manioc cakes and as much food as you could want. Don't be afraid. Come down!"

This time the boy climbed all the way down. He sat on the jaguar's neck and rode with him to where the animal lived.

The Boy Meets the Jaguar's Wife

The jaguar's wife was waiting. She would cook all the wild game for her husband and herself.

"Who's that boy? Why are you bringing him here?" asked the jaguar's wife.

"This boy was in the forest sitting on top of a large rock. I brought him home to be our son," answered the jaguar.

"We need all the food for ourselves," she said. "We do not need a son." The jaguar's wife did not like the idea of another mouth to feed. She wanted it all for the two of them.

At last, though, the jaguar persuaded his wife to keep the boy. So the boy stayed with the jaguars.

In the jaguars' house was a burning fire, where meat was cooked. The jaguars had meat from tapir, boar, and other animals. They also had manioc cakes and sweet potatoes. The boy had a big appetite. The jaguar always gave the boy most of the food.

The jaguar told his wife, "You must always be good to the boy. You must give him whatever he wants to eat, even when I'm away. You must not ever scare him."

Still the wife was not very happy to give away so much food.

One day, the jaguar went hunting. Before he left, he told the boy to eat the roasted tapir if he got hungry. The jaguar's wife did not like hearing this.

Later on, the boy went to the fire. On the hot stones by the fire were roasted boar and roasted tapir wrapped in banana leaves. The boy picked up the tapir meat and started to unwrap it.

The jaguar's wife yelled, "Don't eat the tapir! My husband told you to eat the boar meat." She took the tapir meat away from the boy.

"No," said the boy. "He told me to eat the tapir, and I will do as I please."

"No, he did not!" yelled the jaguar's wife.

"You will not eat at all."

The two argued. Finally, the boy grabbed the tapir meat and ate it anyway. The jaguar's wife became very angry. She showed her teeth and claws and growled at the boy. Then she crouched down as if getting ready to jump on him.

The boy screamed and ran into the forest to find the jaguar. When he found the big cat, the boy told the jaguar that his wife had tried to scare him. Then the boy and the jaguar returned home.

Entering the house, the jaguar was angry. He said to his wife, "I told you not to scare the boy. I mean it. Don't ever frighten him again. Give him whatever he wants."

Another day, however, the boy and the wife argued again. This time, when the boy went running for help, the jaguar made a bow and some arrows for him.

"This must stop," said the jaguar. "I am giving you this strong bow and these sharp arrows. If my wife scares you again, shoot and kill her."

Then the jaguar taught the boy how to use the bow and arrows. He showed him how to aim for the heart when shooting.

"After you kill my wife, we will leave

here," the jaguar told the boy. "I'll show you how to get back to your village, and I will live in the forest."

Not long after this, the jaguar again left the boy with his wife while he went hunting. As usual, the boy went to the fireplace. There lay large piles of roasted tapir and boar wrapped in banana leaves. The jaguar's wife was sitting across the room spinning cotton thread. Right away, she started to tell the boy which meat he could eat. They yelled and argued.

The boy hid behind the piles of meat so that the jaguar's wife could not see him. He took the bow in one hand, and with the other hand he drew an arrow. The jaguar woman started to growl. The boy slowly took aim. Suddenly, the jaguar woman bared her teeth and bent down to jump. The boy leaped from behind the meat and let go of the arrow. The arrow struck the animal's heart, and she fell down. The boy had killed the jaguar's wife.

When the jaguar returned home, the boy told him everything that had happened. Then the boy got ready for his trip home. He took a burning log from the fire and some cotton thread on a spindle. He packed some roasted meat and manioc cakes. Then the jaguar pointed out the way for the boy.

"In that direction, far away, is your village," the jaguar said. "I will go the other way, deep into the forest."

So the boy started for home, and the jaguar went the opposite way.

The Boy Returns Home

The boy walked for a long time. The sun was setting when he saw his village on the other side of a river.

The boy was not sure his people would know him. He had lived with the jaguars a long time.

That night the boy slept in the forest. The next morning, feeling braver, he walked up to his house. His family was overjoyed.

The boy told his family all that had happened. He showed them the roasted meat, the burning log, and the cotton thread on the spindle.

His father took the boy to the middle of the village. Once again, the boy described his life with the jaguars. He told the villagers that the jaguars had many wonderful things. The people had not heard of these things before.

"The jaguars had a fire that burned all

the time. They cooked food on the fire, and the food tasted much better than ours. The jaguars also had foods we don't have. They had this cotton thread, which they used for sewing," said the boy.

Then one of the men said, "Let's go to the jaguar's house now! Let's get these things!"

The others agreed, so the men and the boys of the village started on the trip. To get there quickly, they changed into wild animals. They became tapirs, boars, deer, and birds. They all followed the young boy.

When they got to the jaguar's home, they kept very quiet. They slowly crept up to the front. They looked inside to make sure that the jaguar was not there. When they were certain the jaguar was gone, the villagers went inside.

There in the jaguar's home, the villagers found all that the boy had described. There was a fire in the fireplace. There were manioc cakes, roasted meat, bananas, and sweet potatoes. There was also a spindle with cotton thread.

The villagers took all the food they could carry. They took the spindle with the thread. Each person also took a burning log.

When they got back to the village, the

people changed themselves back into men and boys.

The people were quite happy to have all the things the jaguar had. Now they would always have fire for roasting meat and baking manioc cakes. They would have bananas and sweet potatoes. They would know how to spin cotton thread for sewing.

The villagers thanked the boy. These things from the jaguar changed their lives forever.

1. *Where did the jaguar find the young boy?*
2. *Why did the boy kill the jaguar's wife?*
3. *Why did the men and boys go to the jaguar's house?*

The Man Who Made the Plains

This story comes from the Cuiva of Colombia. It explains how savannas came to be. Savannas are large areas of flat, grassy land. They are like the plains of North America.

Long ago there was only jungle as far as you could see. There was no savanna.

At this time a man named Mare lived in the jungle with his family. One day, Mare climbed a tall tree near his house. From the treetop, he looked out over the land. Mare's mother was nearby below the tree working outside the house.

Mare said to his mother, "I see no fields anywhere near here. I am very tired of seeing just the jungle."

"I am tired of the jungle, too," said his mother.

"What do you think we should do, Mother?" said Mare.

"I don't know," she answered.

Mare said, "Maybe I should burn the jungle. I could do that."

"That sounds like a good idea," agreed his mother. She thought Mare would burn just a small part of the jungle.

Very early the next morning, Mare told his mother, "I'm hungry. I want some nuts to eat. Please get me some nuts."

Mare's mother gathered some nuts that the birds had dropped. She took the nuts to Mare, and he began eating them. In a short time, all the nuts were gone, but Mare was still hungry.

"Mother, I need more food," said Mare.

She brought him hearts of palm and more nuts. Mare ate everything she brought.

Then Mare said, "Mother, I need more food."

His mother shook her head, but she went out and found more hearts of palm and more nuts. Mare kept eating hearts of palm and nuts until noon.

Then his mother said to Mare, "Son, your daughter-in-law is hungry. She wants to eat, too. Why don't you save some food for her?"

Mare did not pay any attention to his mother, however. He just kept on eating. His family couldn't believe how much Mare was eating.

The mother spoke to the others in the family. She said, "No matter how much Mare eats, he doesn't get full. He doesn't seem to get tired of eating. How can he eat so much?"

The mother asked Mare for the rock that they used to crack nuts. She tried telling him that others in the family wanted to eat, too. She asked him why he was eating so much. Mare just kept on eating. He did not even stop to answer his mother.

Finally Mare said, "Here is the rock to crack the nuts. Now the rest of you can eat."

Then Mare started drinking water. He kept drinking for a long time. Finally, he stopped.

Then Mare went outside and began to pull up dry flowers with his feet. He used the dry flowers to start a fire and began burning the jungle. Mare's mother watched him start fires all around the house.

"Son, don't do that," his mother yelled. "The fire will burn us all."

"Don't worry, Mother," answered Mare.

Mare would not stop, and he lit many fires. The fires headed away from the house, however, and the family was safe. Mare started off through the jungle. He was away for a long time lighting fires. The sky filled with smoke. Day after day, Mare lit fires. He traveled a long way, burning down the jungle. There were no longer tall trees and thick forests. The land became grassy.

Finally, Mare came back to his family. He walked up to the house, looking thin and dirty.

Mare's mother called to him, "Where have you been? Look at you. Your body is covered with ashes."

Then Mare said, "Mother, I have burned the jungle! Now we will have a drier, grassy place to live."

"You are thin," his mother said.

"I have had no food since I left," he answered. "I have eaten nothing in all this time."

"So is that why you ate so much food before you started out?" his mother asked. "You planned to do nothing but start fires without stopping?"

"Yes," said Mare. "I have been too busy to eat."

"Thank you, my son," his mother said. "You have made a new kind of land for us."

Then Mare and his family could live in the savanna instead of the jungle. Now there are the savannas because Mare burned the jungle.

1. Where did Mare and his family live?
2. Why did Mare want to create a savanna?
3. What did Mare do before he started burning the jungle?

The Bird Woman

This story comes from the Incas of Peru. It tells how a new group of people came to live on the earth after a great flood. In the story, a macaw, a colorful South American bird, becomes the mother of the new people.

Long ago, a flood covered the earth. The water rose and rose until all of the people except two brothers drowned.

The two brothers had climbed a mountain called Huaca-yñan. They watched the water rise. It rose up the sides of the mountain, higher and higher. Then the mountain itself magically grew higher also. The mountaintop remained higher than the rising water. The brothers stayed on top and did not drown.

Finally, the water went down and the land dried. The brothers were hungry from being on the mountain without food. They came down from the mountain to look for food. They could find only a few plants to eat. They took this small amount of food back to the mountain.

There on the mountain, the brothers built a little house. Each day they went down the mountain to search for food. Each night they returned home, tired from their search and still hungry.

One night, when they had climbed back home, the brothers had a surprise. There inside the house was a feast, already cooked and ready to eat. The next day and the next, it happened again. For ten days, the brothers found cooked food when they returned home.

The brothers then thought of how to find out where the food was coming from. On the eleventh day, they decided that the older brother would stay home. He would hide inside the house and wait to see who came with food.

After a time, two birds flew into the house through the open door. They carried large baskets of food. These birds were macaws, but they had the faces of beautiful women.

As the older brother watched, the birds began to cook the food they had brought. The brother watched in amazement for a few minutes. Then he jumped out and tried to grab the macaws. The angry birds grabbed up all the food and flew away.

When the younger brother came home, he found no food. The older brother told about the macaws with the faces of women.

The bird women

"When I tried to catch them, they flew off," he said.

The brothers decided on a new plan. The next day both brothers hid and waited for the birds. They left the door open so the birds could get in. For two days, however, the birds did not come.

At last, on the third day, the birds came back. They flew into the house and started to cook the food as they had before.

The brothers watched and waited. When the macaws had finished cooking, the brothers ran to the door. Quickly they tried to close the door before the birds could fly out.

The birds were angry and tried to escape. The larger bird got out, but the brothers caught the smaller one before she could fly away.

In time, the brothers fell in love with the macaw and made her their wife. The brothers and the macaw had six sons and daughters. They all lived on the mountain for a long time. The macaw had brought food and seeds that the brothers could plant. So they all had food from then on.

They lived happily, and the sons and daughters had their own sons and daughters.

They all looked back to the macaw as a beloved parent.

All people come from the sons and daughters of the macaw and the brothers. For this reason, the macaw is holy, and people wear macaw feathers at special feasts. The mountain Huaca-yñan is a holy mountain because that's where the macaw and the brothers lived.

1. How did the brothers live through the flood?
2. What surprise did the brothers find at home each night?
3. Why is the macaw holy?

The Man Who Caught Too Many Fish

The story told here comes from the Kariña of Venezuela. It tells about an underwater world where spirits with great powers live. The chief of these spirits is the anaconda, a large South American snake.

Day after day a fisherman caught fish along the banks of a river. He caught so many fish that the water spirits became angry.

One day the water spirits decided to punish the man. As the man was fishing on the riverbank, the water suddenly rose up on his legs. Then a wave covered him all up. The water spirits changed the fisherman into a water creature while he stood there on the riverbank.

At that moment, a voice told the fisherman's wife and children what had happened. They rushed to where the man had been fishing. The man did not want his family to see him as a water creature. Quickly he slid deep into the river. There he began to live a new life as a water spirit.

After a while, the man who was now a

water spirit wanted to be like the others around him. He wanted to have a water spirit for a wife.

The one he chose was the daughter of the fish master. She agreed, and they were married. For a year, the man lived with his new wife.

After a year, though, the man began to miss his human family. So he asked the fish master, the great anaconda, if he could visit his human wife and children. He promised that after a visit, he would return to his water family.

"Yes, you may go," said the anaconda. "Remember this, though. There are two things your human family must not do. Your wife or children must not paint you to protect you against spirits. Also, they must not see your face at night. If they do either of these two things, you cannot return to the water world."

The man went to his old home, where he became a human again. His wife and children were very happy to see him.

That night as the man lay down to sleep, he turned into a water creature again. He remembered the words of the fish master and called out to his children.

"There are two things you must not do, my children," he said. "Do not paint me. Also, do not bring a light toward me. If you see me or paint me, I cannot return to my water family."

"All right," the children called back.

The oldest son lay awake thinking. "If I paint my father," he thought, "he can't return to the water. Then my father will stay here. I will do it!"

The boy got up in the night. He carried a light and walked softly to where his father slept. He held the light up close. There he saw a large water creature where his father had been. Working gently, the boy painted the face of his father the water creature.

The next morning, the father woke up and felt the paint. He became very angry.

"I told you not to do this!" he yelled. "You looked at me in the night. You painted my face. Now the anaconda will never let me go back to live underwater."

After saying this, the man disappeared. His family never saw him again.

The Man Who Caught Too Many Fish 71

1. *Why was the fisherman changed into a water spirit?*
2. *What warning did the fish master give the man before he returned home?*
3. *Why did the son disobey his father?*

The Otter Woman

> This story from the Cuiva of Colombia explains where the first otter came from. It tells about a woman who turns into an otter. In many South American myths, people change into animals and animals change into people.

Far up the river, there was a beautiful woman who was very good at catching fish.

One day the woman was cooking the fish she had caught that day. Her husband could not understand how she had gotten so many fish. He became angry and jealous. He said, "Another man must have given you these fish."

"No!" the woman answered. "I myself caught these fish."

"You have to be lying!" said her husband.

"No," she said. "I am telling you the truth. I can catch fish whenever I want to. I am good at fishing."

So her husband said no more that day.

The next day, the woman went to get water and again brought home fish. Again, her husband became angry with her, saying the fish must have come from another man.

"No, I tell you. I caught these fish myself," she said.

Then her husband left to find other food, and the woman cooked the fish.

Another day, the woman asked her sister-in-law, her husband's sister, to come fishing with her. The sister-in-law often went with the woman to fish.

The two women walked to a large lake that was full of waves.

"Sister-in-law, wait for me here," said the woman as she dived into the lake. After swimming all around the lake under the water, the woman came back. She brought several fish she had caught.

"The lake is full of fish," she said when she climbed ashore. "I could catch many more of them."

"Then keep on fishing," the sister-in-law answered. She took the fish to get them ready to cook.

The woman went back again and again. She caught more and more fish.

After a while, the sister-in-law said, "You must stop now. We have plenty of fish."

The woman kept on fishing anyway. She liked catching the fish even after she had enough of them. Finally, the woman came out of the water and started a fire to cook the fish.

While she cooked, she told her sister-in-law about how her husband had been acting. "Your brother does not treat me well," said the woman.

Just then the husband came to the camp. Upon seeing so many fish, he got very angry once again.

The man yelled at his wife. "You are getting these fish from another man!" he said.

"No, I am not," answered the woman. "I am tired of hearing you say that."

The sister-in-law spoke up. "Brother," she said, "stop talking like that to your wife! If you don't stop, she will leave you. She will become an animal who stays in the water and catches fish."

The man kept on yelling. After listening for a while, the wife dived back into the lake.

As she swam deeper into the water, the woman began to turn into an animal. She became an otter, which is a water animal that is very good at catching fish.

After that, the woman lived as an otter, swimming and fishing all day.

The sister-in-law and the husband no

longer had many fish to eat. They often went hungry because the woman who had caught their fish had left.

After a time, the otter woman had baby otters. Then the lake, and eventually other lakes and rivers, had many otters.

1. What was the woman good at doing?
2. Why did the husband get angry with his wife?
3. Why did the woman leave her husband?

The Condor's Wife

The condor is a large bird that lives high in the Andes Mountains. This story from Peru tells about a condor that falls in love with a young woman who herds sheep.

The Condor's Visit

A beautiful young woman was watching her flock of sheep as they grazed. A condor saw this woman and fell in love with her. So the condor turned himself into a handsome young man and went to visit the woman.

He walked up to the woman and began talking to her and asking her about her work.

"I am watching my sheep," she answered. "If a fox tries to get one of the lambs, I shoot it with my slingshot. I also shoot at the condor who tries to grab me."

"May I stay here with you and marry you?" the condor man asked. "I will help you scare the fox and the condor away."

"No," the young woman answered. "If you stayed, I would not be free anymore. I love being free and being alone. I love being here

The condor and the woman

with my sheep. I don't want to marry anyone."

The young man left, but he came back the next day. The woman was willing to talk to the man and asked him to tell her about his life.

"I live high in the mountains, near the clouds," the condor man said. "From up there, I am the first to see the sun rise in the morning. I am the last to see it set at night. It is beautiful and quiet there. Why don't you come and live with me? We would enjoy the pure air of the snowy mountain. We would have the sweet smells rising from the flowers in the valley. Please come with me."

"No, I don't want to live on the mountain," the young woman replied. "I love this pasture and my sheep. Besides, I love my mother, too. If I left, my mother would cry."

"All right," said the condor man. "Please do one thing for me, though. My shoulder itches. Maybe if you scratched it for me, the itch would go away."

The woman agreed to do that. The condor man bent over, and the woman leaned over his back. When her hands were on his shoulders, the man changed back into a condor. He flew into the air. The woman had to hold onto his wings so that she wouldn't fall.

The condor flew high up into the sky. He came to land in a cave near the top of a mountain. Many other condors lived in nearby caves. All the condors flapped their wings and shouted with joy when the woman arrived.

Life on the Mountain

At first, the woman was afraid and unhappy. After a while, though, she became happy living with the condor. The condor was always loving toward his wife. However, he never brought her any food. He flew off to get his own food, but he did not bring food home. She couldn't fly to get her own food, and of course, she grew very hungry. She became very thirsty, too.

Finally, the woman told her husband, "I am happy with you, but I can't live just on love. I must have food and water."

The condor agreed to give his wife what she needed. He flew down from the mountain. From the fields he took the meat of dead animals. From gardens he took vegetables. He pecked the mountainside with his beak, and a spring of water poured out.

The condor gave the water and food to his wife. Even though the food was rotting, the hungry woman ate it. She wanted some bread also, but the condor could not find any.

The Parrot's Rescue

Meanwhile, down below, the young woman's mother cried for her daughter. The young woman began to miss her mother also. She grew tired of the condor and of the poor food. She was changing, though, because she had been with the condors so long. She became thin, and she started to grow feathers.

Now a parrot lived nearby the house of the woman's mother. He visited the mother, who was crying. The parrot felt sorry for the woman.

The parrot said to the woman, "Don't cry. I know that your daughter is not dead. She's living high up on a mountain. The condor has made her his wife. I can return her to you, though, if you will let me have some corn from your garden."

The mother agreed.

Then the parrot flew off to the condor's cave. While the condors were away, the parrot grabbed the young woman. He flew with her back to her mother's house.

The young woman appeared thin and smelled of rotten food. Her feathers made her look silly. Her mother was overjoyed to see her anyway. The mother cleaned the young woman and put beautiful clothes on her. The mother and daughter were happy to be together once more.

Meanwhile, the condor returned to his nest and found his wife gone. The condor knew at once that the parrot had taken her, for the parrot often caused trouble. Angry, he searched for the parrot. He found the parrot in the mother's garden, happily eating corn.

The condor grabbed the parrot. "I will kill you," he said. With that he ate the parrot whole.

Even so, the parrot did not die. He passed through the condor's body. The condor ate him again, and the same thing happened again.

Finally, the condor ripped the parrot to pieces and ate the little pieces. This time each piece the condor ate came out as a beautiful little parrot. There were many beautiful parrots.

The sad condor returned home without his wife. In his grief, he dyed his feathers to make them all black. His tears became the ashes that fly in fireplaces.

So the condor's grief brought some things that were colorful as well as some things that were dark. His sadness brought the many colorful parrots that are here today. It also brought the dark ashes that rise above our fires.

1. Why did the condor ask the young woman to scratch his back?
2. How did the young woman get back to her mother's house?
3. What finally happened to the parrot?

The Jaguar's Wife

> *This myth comes from the Chamacoco of Paraguay. It tells about a woman who marries a jaguar. The jaguar was a feared and respected animal. This is another myth in which people and animals cross over into each other's worlds.*

The Jaguar's Trick

A husband and wife went into the forest to hunt for food.

"You look here, and I will go farther on," said the husband.

After he had left his wife, the man found a bee's nest and began collecting the honey from it. Meanwhile, the woman had found some berries and had started picking them.

After a time, the woman called to her husband, "Where are you, my husband? Let's go back now."

"Here I am," came an answer. The woman thought it was her husband who had answered, but it was not. Her husband was far away and had not heard her.

"I must go to where my husband

answered me," thought the woman.

The woman started searching for her husband. As she went, she kept calling him. She thought her husband was answering her, but it was a jaguar that kept answering her calls.

During this time, the husband had started looking for his wife. He called out for her also. After a short time, the husband came upon the jaguar. Seeing the wild cat, the man ran away in fear.

Then the jaguar called to the woman again. "Come, my wife. I've found a lot of fruit over here."

The woman, thinking her husband was calling her, hurried toward the voice. She found a tree loaded with fruit and quickly climbed it to pick the fruit.

Just then the jaguar came out from behind a bush and sat under the tree. When the woman looked down and saw the jaguar, she started to cry.

"Please do not cry," said the jaguar. "I do not want to eat you. No, I want you to come with me and be my wife."

The woman was afraid not to do as the jaguar asked. She let the jaguar take her to his village. There were many jaguars living there, but there were no other people.

Meanwhile, the man had run back to his village.

"What has happened to your wife?" asked the people in the village.

"She got lost," answered the man. Then he told the people how he had seen a jaguar and had run away.

The man and the other villagers began to search the forest for the woman. Soon they found the woman's footprints and followed them. After a while, the woman's footprints were surrounded by the footprints of many jaguars.

Because the people feared these wild cats, they went back home. The man had to give up on finding his wife.

The Son's Plan

Now the man and woman had a son. As he grew up, he became a good hunter. One day, when hunting in the forest, the son shot an arrow at a bird.

The bird flew from one branch to another. As it flew, it called out, "Your mother lives here in the forest."

When the boy got back home, he asked his father, "What happened to my mother?"

"A long time ago, my son, a jaguar took your mother," the man answered.

"Please make an axe for me," the boy said. "I will search the forest for my mother, and I will bring her back."

"There is no use, my son," the father said. "You will not find her. The forest is full of jaguars, and you will be in great danger."

"I must go. I must find her. When I do, I will kill the jaguars," said the son.

The father did not want his son to go. He knew jaguars were very dangerous and could easily kill the boy.

"No," the father said. "It is the jaguars that will kill you."

Because the boy begged to go, the man finally agreed. He made an axe and wove a basket for the boy.

The boy was very sure of himself. "I will return with a basket full of jaguar tails," he said.

That day the boy went into the forest and traveled far, but he found nothing. The next day and the next, he traveled farther and farther. Finally, he found an old jaguar camp. He saw human footprints and knew they belonged to his mother. Although the tracks were old, he could still see where they went.

The boy followed the footprints to another camp. This camp was not an old one. A fire still smoked in that camp.

"Soon I will find them," thought the boy.

In the morning, the boy started out again. He came upon fresh tracks.

"They must be close," the boy thought.

Since it was nearly noon, the boy sat down to rest for a while. Just then, he saw a fire up ahead. Crawling toward the fire, he saw his mother sitting alone on a mat. He was surprised at how his mother looked. She had started to look like a jaguar. She had jaguar fur on her head and her belly and her back.

Inching closer and closer, the boy whispered, "Mother, it is your son. I will rescue you."

Jaguar Tails

The mother turned toward her son. She was glad to see him, but she was also worried. "Why did you come?" she said. "My jaguar husband will kill you."

"Don't worry," the boy answered. "With this axe, I will kill all the jaguars. You can come home and be with my father and me."

His mother did want to go home. She

agreed to help her son. She explained, "The jaguars are out hunting now. They don't all return together. They come back one by one."

Even from far away, the jaguars could smell the scent of another human back in their camp. They began calling one another, "A man is in the camp. Let's go back now and eat him."

The woman could hear the jaguars' calls. She yelled back at them, "There is no man here." Then she helped her son hide.

The first jaguar entered the camp and sniffed around. Then the jaguar said, "Why did you say there was no man here? I know I smell a man."

"I'll show you," the woman answered. "There is no man here."

The jaguar searched the camp but found nothing.

Now it was the custom for each jaguar to wear three helmets while out hunting. The helmets were made of reeds and clay. The jaguars always took these caps off in camp where they were safe.

"Come here," the woman said to the first jaguar. "I'll take the helmets off your head."

After the woman removed the helmets, she called her son. The boy rushed upon the jaguar. He hit the big cat on the head with his axe and killed him. Then he cut off the animal's tail. He threw the body far into the forest.

One by one, the other jaguars came home. The mother and the son did the same thing to each one. Finally, the woman's husband, the largest jaguar, returned.

"I smell a man!" he roared.

"Come. I'll show you there is no man here," his wife answered.

The jaguar looked around and found nothing. Then the wife started to take off his three helmets. She could get only two off, however.

The boy had begun to wonder what was taking so long. Finally, he rushed out from his hiding spot before the woman called him.

The jaguar still had one helmet on when the woman's son came to kill him. The boy hit the jaguar as hard as he could, but the blow did not kill the animal. The big cat ran into the forest.

"I'll go after him," the boy said.

Seeing the jaguar escape gave the mother time to think about what it would mean to kill him. After all, she had come to like him, and she had lived as his wife.

Removing the jaguar's helmets

"No!" she said. "Forget about him. You will not be able to kill him."

The boy took his mother's advice. He put all the jaguar tails in his basket. Then he said to his mother, "Let's go now. Let's return home."

That night the woman missed her jaguar husband. She ran away from the boy and went to find the jaguar.

In the morning, the boy went back to his village. He took the jaguar tails along to prove what he had done. Before walking into the village, he hid the jaguar tails in the forest. He would go for them later.

As he entered the village, the boy called the people together. He told them about all that had happened, but the people would not believe him.

"You did not see any jaguars!" they said, laughing at him.

"I thought you would not believe me," the boy said. "I have brought proof." Then the boy went to get the basket of jaguar tails. When he got back, he took the tails out and handed them to the people to pass around.

"See for yourselves," the boy told them. "I did try to rescue my mother. I did kill the jaguars. I could not rescue my mother, though. She went back to her jaguar husband. She has become a jaguar. She already has jaguar fur on her head and on her belly and on her back."

The woman stayed in the forest with her jaguar husband. The son did not try again to find her or to kill the large jaguar. The woman and the jaguar became parents. Because the woman stayed with the jaguar in the forest, jaguars exist there today.

1. *How did the jaguar get the woman to climb the tree?*
2. *Why didn't the boy kill the last jaguar?*
3. *How did the boy prove that he had killed the jaguars?*

The Rabbit's Trick

This story comes from the Warao of Guyana. It tells about a rabbit who plays a trick on some hunters. Stories likes this one are called trickster tales. In such tales, animals play tricks on one another or on people.

Rabbit did not like to work, but he did like to eat. He tried to think of ways that he could eat without working for his food.

One morning, Rabbit was very hungry. He sat at the bottom of a high, overhanging cliff. He decided to wait to see if someone with food would pass by.

After a short time, Rabbit saw a group of hunters coming his way. They were carrying some game that they had killed. Rabbit wanted their game for his dinner. He thought of a plan.

Rabbit grabbed a long log. He pressed one end of the log against the side of the cliff. He braced the other end against the ground. As Rabbit was pushing the log into place, the hunters came by.

"Why are you pushing on that log, Rabbit?" one of the hunters asked.

Rabbit answered, "Can't you see? The mountain is leaning over. I must brace it up, or it will fall. We could all be killed. Look up! Don't you see how the mountain is moving?"

The hunters looked up at the mountain. Clouds were passing over the mountain. The moving clouds caused the hunters to think they saw the mountain moving.

"Please hold this log for me!" Rabbit said. "I need a rest! I have been holding up the mountain all morning."

The hunters put down their game. All together, they pushed against the log. They kept on pushing for hours. Finally, the sun was about to go down. The hunters were so tired they could not push any longer.

"If the mountain falls, we can't help it," said one of the hunters. "We just can't keep this up any longer."

The hunters let go of the log and looked around to find their game. Their game was gone, though—and so was Rabbit!

Rabbit had tricked the hunters out of their game. He had a fine dinner that he had not done a bit of work for. His plan had worked perfectly.

The hunters holding up the mountain

1. Why did Rabbit say he was pressing the log against the mountain?
2. Why did the hunters agree to hold the log for Rabbit?
3. Who took the hunters' game?

The Red Birds

This trickster tale comes from the Mataco of Argentina. The main trickster in this story is Takjuaj, a creature who has great powers. Takjuaj can take the form of a person or any kind of animal. He appears in many Mataco stories.

One day Takjuaj began to feel thirsty and hungry. Then he saw an old woman sitting outside her house. The woman was rocking a baby, her grandson. The grandmother was actually a wasp in the form of a human. Takjuaj walked up to the woman. He saw some jars of water near the house.

"May I have some water to drink?" Takjuaj asked the old woman.

"We have many water jars here. You may have one," the old woman answered. She pointed toward the jars.

Takjuaj took a sip from each jar.

"All the water is warm," said Takjuaj. "I would like some cool water from the stream. Will you get some for me?"

"Yes, I will," said the woman. She put the baby in a swing. Then she picked up an empty jar and walked toward the stream.

Takjuaj eyed the baby and said, "Now I shall eat!"

Then Takjuaj said a few magic words, which made it impossible for the woman to fill her jar. At the stream, the woman kept dipping the jar, but it did not fill up.

Meanwhile, Takjuaj cooked the baby in a pot and ate the boy. Afterwards, he drank some water. Then he placed a rock in the baby's swing. No longer hungry or thirsty, Takjuaj left the house. Again he said some magic words so that the woman could now fill her jar.

The old woman came back from the stream with the full jar. She saw the used cooking pot and the rock in the swing.

"That man tricked me! He has eaten my grandson!" she screamed. "I will make him sorry for this."

The old woman knew that Takjuaj would lie down for a nap after eating. She took some wax and went searching for him. Soon she found him sleeping under a tree. She stuffed the wax in his eyes, ears, nose, and mouth. Then she went back home.

After a while, Takjuaj woke up from his nap. He could not see or hear or smell or open his mouth. He thought about what to do. Using magic, he called the birds of the forest. Many birds came to help him.

"Remove this wax!" he ordered the birds.

The birds pecked and pecked at the wax, but they could not get it out.

The birds asked one another, "What can we do? Is there any bird who isn't here? Is there any bird who can do this job?"

One of the birds said, "The woodpecker is not here! Surely the woodpecker can get the wax out."

So the birds called the woodpecker, and the woodpecker came. With one peck, the little bird removed the wax in Takjuaj's mouth. As the wax came out, blood squirted over some of the birds. The woodpecker kept on and pulled the wax from Takjuaj's eyes, ears, and nose.

Takjuaj's blood colored the feathers of some birds. These birds turned red. Some dark blood fell on other birds. They became black.

This is how some birds came to have red feathers. Ravens are black because dark blood covered them.

Takjuaj was unkind in tricking the wasp. Still, some good came of his bad deed. Today there are beautiful red birds and beautiful black birds.

1. *How did Takjuaj make the wasp woman stay at the stream?*
2. *Why did the grandmother plug up Takjuaj's eyes, ears, nose, and mouth?*
3. *How did some birds come to have red feathers?*

Pronunciation Guide

Every effort has been made to present native pronunciations of the unusual names in this book. Sometimes experts differed in their opinions, however, or no pronunciation could be found. Also, certain foreign-language sounds were felt to be unpronounceable by today's readers. In these cases, editorial license was exercised in selecting pronunciations.

Key

The letter or letters used to show pronunciation have the following sounds:

a	as in *map* and *glad*
ah	as in *pot* and *cart*
aw	as in *fall* and *lost*
ch	as in *chair* and *child*
e	as in *let* and *care*
ee	as in *feet* and *please*
ey	as in *play* and *face*
g	as in *gold* and *girl*
hy	as in *huge* and *humor*
i	as in *my* and *high*
ih	as in *sit* and *clear*

j	as in *jelly* and *gentle*
k	as in *skill* and *can*
ky	as in *cute*
l	as in *long* and *pull*
my	as in *mule*
ng	as in *sing* and *long*
ny	as in *canyon* and *onion*
o	as in *slow* and *go*
oo	as in *cool* and *move*
ow	as in *cow* and *round*
s	as in *soon* and *cent*
sh	as in *shoe* and *sugar*
th	as in *thin* and *myth*
u	as in *put* and *look*
uh	as in *run* and *up*
y	as in *you* and *yesterday*
z	as in *zoo* and *pairs*

Guide

Capital letters are used to represent stressed syllables. For example, the word *ugly* would be written here as "UHG lee."

Ayoreo: ah yo REY o

Bororo: bo RO ro

Carib: KAH rihb

Cayapo: KAH yah po

Chamacoco: chah mah KO ko

cipoi: SEE po ee

Coya: KO yah

criollos: kree O yos

Cuiva: koo EE vah

Cuzco: KOOS ko

Guyana: gee AH nah

hima-heru: EE mah EY roo

Huaca-yñan: wah kah ee NYAN

Inca: IHN kah

Kariña: kah REE nyah

manioc: MAN ee ahk

Mare: MAH rey

Mataco: mah TAH ko

No-hi-ha-basi: no ee ah BAH see

Orinoco: o ree NO ko

Paraparawa: pah rah pah RAH wah

plantain: PLAN tin

savanna: sah VAN ah

shaman: SHAHM en

Takjuaj: tak choo AHCH

Tiahuanacan: TEE ah wah nah kuhn

Tiahuanaco: TEE ah wah nah ko

Titicaca: tee tee KAH kah

Tohurato: to oo RAH to

Trio: TREE o

Viracocha: weer ah KO chah

Waraku: wah RAH koo

Warao: wah RAH o

Yaruro: yah ROO ro